GREETING THE DAY

GREETING THE DAY

Morning Prayers and Meditations from Around the World

Brian Wright

Adams Media Corporation
HOLBROOK, MASSACHUSETTS

Published by
Adams Media Corporation
260 Center Street, Holbrook, MA 02343

ISBN: 1-58062-121-X

Printed in the United States of America.

J I H G F E D C B A

Library of Congress Cataloging-in-Publication Data

Greeting the day: morning prayers and meditations from around
the world / [compiled by] Brian Wright.
p. cm.
ISBN 1-58062-121-X
1. Prayers. I. Wright, Brian.
BL560.G74   1999
291.4'33—dc21   98-31836
CIP

Cover Illustration:
©1998, Mary Worcester/Gretchen Harris Associates.

This book is available at quantity discounts for bulk purchases.
For information, call 1-800-872-5627 (in Massachusetts, 781-767-8100).

Visit our home page at http://www.adamsmedia.com

Table of Contents

Foreword

AWAKENING TO A NEW MORNING FROM A SOUL-REFRESHING NIGHT OF SLEEP IS A TIMELESS AND UNTARNISHED GIFT—A GIFT WITHOUT RELIGIOUS OR HISTORICAL BORDERS. We emerge from the realm of dreams with a fresh perspective on the simplest things in life. The song of a bird or the sun pouring in through the windows is received with an intimacy and an immediacy. It is during this time of waking that many mystics, monks, and poets have found their inspiration. Many of their results are in this book.

On some mornings, when we are refreshed and eager to meet the challenges and fortunes of the new day, it's easy to be thankful. On others, though, when the weight of the world rests upon our shoulders, we may feel a need to ask for the divine support and strength of our God. In these prayers, you'll find evidence that pain, struggle, and a need for reassurance has always been a part of human experience.

The ritual of spending a few quiet moments soon after rising can help us to become calm and peaceful during the day. In monasteries, as well as in earlier cultures, this early morning time has been considered sacred, a time when a person can become one with the world and the moment. You'll find some of these moments recorded in this book.

We all know that how we begin our morning can effect the remains of the day significantly. If we start our day with the desire to contribute to others and to accomplish worthwhile goals, we soon find that we not only help the world but also enjoy greater peace of mind. Several of the prayers and meditations in this book will help you get your day off to such a productive and positive start. Many of the shorter entries are intended as starting points for further contemplation and meditation.

I offer this collection of morning prayers, meditations, and poems not only to share the insight and wisdom of people of all ages, cultures, and religions but also to show the commonality of our connection to God.

The entries in this anthology were culled exhaustively from holy texts, works by contemporary writers, historical and religious archives, and poetry collections. I hope that you find this collection useful and inspiring—and that it moves you to greet the day more wholeheartedly.

Brian Wright

Gratitude

1

God, my friend,
Thank you for giving me the chance
to live another day,
to work toward my goals,
to make right my wrong doings,
to learn something new,
and to give something back to you.

—BRIAN WRIGHT

2

O Lord our God, the morning is here.
Thou who hast chased the slumber from
        our eyes,
and once more assembled us
to lift up our hands to Thee in praise,
accept our prayers and supplications,
and give us faith and love.
Bless our going out and coming in,
our thoughts, words, and works,
and let us begin this day
with the praise of the unspeakable sweetness
of Thy mercy.

—GREEK LITURGY

3

O our mother the earth, O our father the sky,
Your children are we, and with tired backs
We bring you gifts that you love.
Then weave for us a garment of brightness;
May the warp be the white light of morning,
May the weft be the red light of evening,
May the fringes be the falling rain,
May the border be the standing rainbow.
Thus weave for us a garment of brightness
That we may walk fittingly where birds sing,
That we may walk fittingly where grass is green,
O our mother the earth, O our father the sky!

—TEWA "SONG OF THE SKY LOOM"

4

Lord, I am happy this morning.
Birds and angels sing and I am exultant.
The universe and our hearts
are open to your grace.
I feel my body and give thanks.
The sun burns my skin and I thank you.
The breakers are rolling toward the seashore,
the sea foam splashes our house.
I give thanks.

—MORNING PRAYER, GHANA

5

O sun behind all suns
Let all creation praise you
Let the daylight
and the shadows praise you
Let the fertile earth
and the swelling sea praise you
Let the winds and the rain,
the lightning and the thunder
praise you
Let all that breathes,
both male and female, praise you
And I shall praise you.
O God of all life
I give you greeting this day.

—J. PHILIP NEWELL

6

O wonderful!
The sun arises,
and all the world is lighted.
So wakes the mind to truth,
and man,
benighted in error,
sees its brightness,
and adores.

—FROM THE AVATANSAKA SUTRA

7

At dawn do I sing the praise
for that which is unreachable
by the mind and words,
but by whose grace all worlds shine.

—Hindu morning prayer

8

*O Thou
who hast made me to feel
the morning wind upon my limbs,
help me to feel Thy presence
as I bow in worship of Thee.*

—CHANDRA DEVANESEN

9

*Good morning, Guvnor,
and thank you.*

—AN ANONYMOUS
HOSPITAL PORTER'S PRAYER

10

The sun is shining . . . thank you Lord.
I mean it is shining:
the sky and everything is warm and smiling.
But it is not only that . . . my heart is smiling.
I know that I am loved . . . and that I love too.
Thank you, Lord, the sun is shining.

—MICHAEL HOLLINGS AND ETTA GULLICK

11

From the East to the West,
from the North to the South,
all nations and peoples
bless the creator of creatures with
*   a new blessing.*
For He made the light of the sun
rise today over the world.

—ARMENIAN HYMN

12

God's mercies are new every morning.

—FROM LAMENTATIONS 3

13

Today, like every other day,
we wake up empty and frightened.
Don't open the door to the study
and begin reading.
Take down a musical instrument.
Let the beauty we love be what we do.
There are hundreds of ways
to kneel and kiss the ground.

—RUMI

14

Listen to the exhortation of the dawn!
Look to this day!
For it is life,
the very Life of Life.
In its brief course
lie all the Varieties
and Realities of your Existence;
The Bliss of Growth,
The Glory of Action,
The Splendor of Beauty,
For Yesterday is but a Dream,
and Tomorrow is only a Vision;
But Today well lived
Makes every Yesterday
a dream of happiness,

And every Tomorrow
a vision of Hope.
Look well therefore to this Day!
Such is the salutation of the Dawn.

—Hindu "Salutation of the Dawn"

15

Lord, my joys mount as do the birds,
heavenward.
The night has taken wings
and I rejoice in the light.
What a day, Lord! What a day!

—MORNING PRAYER, GHANA

16

The magpie! The magpie!
Here underneath
In the white of his wings
On the footsteps of morning.
It dawns! It dawns!

—TEWA PRAYER

17

When you arise in the morning,
give thanks for the morning light,
for your life and strength.
Give thanks for your food
and the joy of living.
If you see no reason for giving thanks,
the fault lies in yourself.

—TECUMSEH

18

Waking up this morning, I see the blue sky.
I join my hands in thanks
for the many wonders of life;
for having twenty-four brand-new hours
*   before me.*
The sun is rising.
The forest becomes my awareness
bathed in the sunshine.
I walked across a field of sunflowers.
Tens of thousands of flowers are turned
toward the bright east.
My awareness is like the sun.
My hands are sowing seeds for the next harvest.
My ear is filled with the sound of the
*   rising tide.*
In the magnificent sky, clouds are approaching

with joy from many directions.
I can see the fragrant lotus ponds of my
     homeland.
I can see coconut trees along the rivers.
I can see rice fields stretching, stretching,
laughing at the sun and rain.
Mother Earth gives us coriander,
basil, celery, and mint.
Tomorrow the hills and mountains of the
     country
will be green again.
Tomorrow the buds of life will spring up quickly.
Folk poetry will be as sweet as the songs of
     children.

—THICH NHAT HANH

19

The morning comes and now is!
Welcome the day with gladness,
And greet the dawn with praise!

—CONGREGATION OF ABRAXAS

20

All night the gods were with us,
Now night is gone;
Silence the rattle,
Sing the daybreak song,
For in the dawn Bluebird calls,
And out from his blankets of tumbled gray
The Sun comes, combing his hair for the day.

—AMERICAN INDIAN PRAYER

21

All that is in the heavens and in the earth glorifieth God.
He causes the night to pass into the day,
and He causes the day to pass into the night,
and He is the knower of all that is.

—THE KORAN

22

i thank You God for most this amazing
day:for the leaping greenly spirits of trees
and a blue true dream of sky;and for everything
which is natural which is infinite which is yes
(i who have died am alive again today,
and this is the sun's birthday;this is the birth
day of life and of love and wings:and of the gay
great happening illimitably earth)
how should tasting touching hearing seeing
breathing any—lifted from the no
of all nothing—human merely being
doubt unimaginable you?
(now the ears of my ears awake and
now the eyes of my eyes are opened)

—E. E. CUMMINGS

23

Father-Creator,
Provider-from-of-old,
Ancient-of days,
fresh-born from the womb of night are we.
In the first dawning of the new day
draw we nigh unto thee.
Forlorn are the eyes till they've seen the Chief.

—SOUTH AFRICAN PRAYER

24

Awakening
in a moment of peace
I give thanks
to the source of all peace.
As I set forth
into the day
the birds sing
with new voices
and I listen
with new ears
and give thanks.
You can see forever
when the vision is clear.
In this moment
each moment
I give thanks.

—HARRIET KOFALK

25

The sun is shining
the sky is blue
Shall we go out
in the world today
The air is sweet
The day is new
Adventure is only
a footstep away
There are drums to be played
There are bells to be rung
There are thousands of
Heart-lifting songs to be sung
Shall we ring them?
Shall we sing them?
To the beat of the drum?

—KIRSTEN SAVITRI BERGH

26

This light is come, amid all lights the fairest;
born is the brilliant, far-extending brightness.
Night, sent away for the sun's uprising,
hath yielded up a birthplace for the morning.

—The Rig-Veda

27

When I rise up
let me rise up joyful
like a bird.

—WENDELL BERRY

28

May the Sun rise well!
May the earth appear
Brightly shone upon.

—SIOUX PRAYER

Protection

29

God, my friend,
I'm going to need you
to look out for me today.
All of my best is not going to be enough.
Whenever I've needed you before,
you've always answered my call.
I know that today
will be no different.

—BRIAN WRIGHT

30

The Sun is dawning,
The Stars are dwindling.
The soul is dawning,
And dreams are dwindling.
Day, then, receive me,
Day, then, protect me,
Walking through earthly life.

—RUDOLF STEINER

31

O Lord, support us all the day long,
until the shadows lengthen and the
evening comes,
and the busy world is hushed,
and the fever of life is over,
and our work is done.
Then in your mercy grant us
a safe lodging,
and a holy rest,
and peace at the last.

—JOHN HENRY NEWMAN

32

We rise up in the morning
before the day,
to betake ourselves to our labor,
to prepare our harvest.
Protect us from the dangerous animal
and from the serpent,
and from every stumbling block.

—AFRICAN MORNING PRAYER

33

Father in heaven!
When the thought of you wakes in our hearts,
let it not awaken like a frightened bird
that flies about in dismay,
but like a child waking from its sleep
with a heavenly smile.

—SOREN KIERKEGAARD

34

Living Lord,
you have watched over me,
and put your hand on my head
during the long, dark hours of night.
Your holy angels have protected me
from all harm and pain.
To you, Lord, I owe life itself.
Continue to watch over me and bless me
during the hours of the day.

—JAKOB BOEHME

35

Morning has risen;
God, take away from us every pain,
Every ill,
Every mishap;
God, let us come safely home.

—NANDI WOMEN'S MORNING PRAYER,
 KENYA

36

O God, I enter in the morning in need of Thee,
powerless and unable to avoid what I dislike,
and incapable of accomplishing what I want,
except with Thy help.
O God, I enter the morning pledged
for what I have done.
Everything is in Thy hand.
I am most in need of Thee,
and Thou are most independent of any being.
Make not, O God, my enemies to gloat
over me.
Protect my friends from any misfortune
and me from the misfortunes of unbelief.
Let me not be concerned with worldly
endeavor.

I pray that on Judgment Day I will have been worthy of Thy sanction through Thy mercy. O God, Thou art the most merciful of the merciful.

—DRUZE PRAYER

37

O God, you have let me pass the night
   in peace,
Let me pass the day in peace.
Wherever I may go
Upon my way which you made peaceable
   for me,
O God, lead my steps.
When I have spoken,
Keep falsehood away from me.
When I am hungry,
Keep me from murmuring.
When I am satisfied,
keep me from pride.
Calling upon you, I pass the day,
O Lord who has no Lord.

—BORAN PRAYER, KENYA

38

Po! God, may the day dawn well;
May you spit upon us the medicine
So that we may walk well!

—Vugusu prayer, Kenya

39

Great mystery of sleep,
Which has safely brought us to the beginning
of this day
We thank you for the refreshment you daily
*   provide,*
And for the renewing cycle of your dreams
Which shelter our fantasies, nourish our
*   vision,*
and purge our angers and fears.
We bless you for providing a new beginning
Whose perennial grace is tangible hope
for all the children of the earth.
We praise the gift of another morning,
And pray that we may be worthy bearers of its
*   trust*
in the hours to come.

May life protect us and surprise us
And be no more harsh than our spirits may
　　bear
Until we rest again in the vast emptiness
of your everlasting arms.

—CONGREGATION OF ABRAXAS

40

Dear God,
how glad we are
that we don't hold you,
but that you hold us!

—HAITIAN PRAYER

Rejuvenation

41

God, my friend,
Charge me today with your intentions
that they may make me
strong and resolute.
I know that true power
can only come from good—
greed, envy, hate and ignorance
are all drains through which
our power can leave us.
Make me strong.

—BRIAN WRIGHT

42

Now this day,
my sun father,
Now that you have come out
standing to your sacred place,
That from which we draw the
water of life,
Prayer meal
Here I give you.
Your long life,
Your old age,
Your waters,
Your seeds,
Your riches,
Your power,
Your strong spirit,
All these to me may you grant.

—ZUNI SUNRISE PRAYER

43

God be in my head,
and in my understanding;
God be in my eyes,
and in my looking;
God be in my mouth,
and in my speaking;
God be in my heart,
and in my thinking;
God be at my end,
and at my departing.

—NEW ZEALAND PRAYER BOOK

44

Yonder comes the dawn,
The universe grows green,
The road to the Underworld
Is open! Yet now we live,
Upward going, upward going!

—TEWA PRAYER

45

"Be cheerful, sir.
Our revels now are ended. These our actors,
As I foretold you, were all spirits and
Are melted into air; into thin air;
And, like the baseless fabric of this vision,
The cloud-capped towers, the gorgeous palaces,
The solemn temples, the great globe itself,
Yea, all which it inherit, shall dissolve,
And, like this insubstantial pageant faded,
Leave not a rack behind. We are such stuff
As dreams are made on, and our little life
Is rounded with a sleep."

—FROM *THE TEMPEST* BY WILLIAM SHAKESPEARE

46

O God who brought me
from the rest of last night
To the new light of this day
Bring me in the new light
of this day
to the guiding light
of the eternal.
Lead me O God
on the journey of justice
Guide me O God
on the pathways of peace
Renew me O God
by the wellsprings of grace
Today, tonight, and forever.

—J. PHILIP NEWELL

47

At dawn may I roam
Against the winds may I roam
At dawn may I roam
When the crow is calling
may I roam.

—SIOUX PRAYER

48

O God, early in the morning I cry to you.
Help me to pray
and to concentrate my thoughts on you:
I cannot do this alone.
In me there is darkness,
But with you there is light;
I am lonely, but you do not leave me;
I am feeble in heart, but with you there is help;
I am restless, but with you there is peace.
In me there is bitterness, but with you there is
     patience;
I do not understand your ways,
But you know the way for me.

Restore me to liberty,
And enable me so to live now
That I may answer before you and before me.
Lord, whatever this day may bring,
Your name be praised.

—DIETRICH BONHOEFFER

49

Quiet the trees; quiet the creepers all.
In the sky's tranquil lap burns the sun's ray.
In my heart's temple doth the silence fall,
Worshiping Thee. Thou, Silent Majestic.
Thou replenishest this tranquil heart.
O Thou Eternal, Absolute,
with silence fill me with song,
In secret, silent, still.

—C. R. DAS

50

The Light of the Sun
Brightens all Space
When dark night is past.
The life of the soul
Now is awakened
From restful Sleep.
O Thou, my soul,
Give thanks to the Light.
In it shines forth
The Power of God.
O thou, my soul,
Be strong for deeds.

—RUDOLF STEINER

51

Dear God, break to me this day
the "bread of life."
My heart is hungry.
Save us from thinking, even for a moment,
that we can feed our souls on things.
Save us from the vain delusion that
the piling up of wealth or comforts can satisfy.
Help us to remember that
the real quest for happiness is within.

—RALPH SPAULDING CUSHMAN

52

The heavens are wide, exceedingly wide.
The earth is wide, very, very wide.
We have lifted it and taken it away.
We have lifted it and brought it back.
From time immemorial,
The God of old bids us all
Abide by his injunctions.
Then shall we get whatever we want,
Be it white or red.
It is God, the Creator, the Gracious One.
Good morning to you, God, good morning.
I am learning, let me succeed.

—AKAN DRUM SONG, GHANA

53

*May the power of God
this day enable me,
the nakedness of God disarm me,
the beauty of God silence me,
the justice of God give me voice,
the integrity of God hold me,
the desire of God move me,
the fear of God expose me to the truth,
the breath of God give me abundant life.*

—JANET MORELY

54

O Lord, grant me to greet
the coming day in peace.
Help me in all things
to rely upon thy holy will.
In every hour of the day
reveal thy will to me.
Bless my dealings
with all who surround me.
Teach me to treat all that comes
to me throughout the day
with peace of soul,
and with firm conviction
that thy will governs all.
In all my deeds and words
guide my thoughts and feelings.

In unforeseen events
let me not forget
that all are sent by thee.
Teach me to act firmly and wisely,
without embittering
or embarrassing others.
Give me strength to bear the fatigue
of the coming day
with all that it shall bring.
Direct my will, teach me to pray,
pray thou thyself in me.

—EASTERN ORTHODOX PRAYER

55

Thanks be to you O God
that I have risen this day
To the rising of this life itself.
May it be a day of blessing,
O God of every gift,
A day of new beginnings given.
Help me to avoid every sin,
and the source of every sin to forsake.
And as the mist scatters
from the crest of the hills,
May each ill haze clear
from my soul O God.

—J. PHILIP NEWELL

56

When the sun rises up,
then the earth, made by God,
becomes clean;
the running waters become clean,
the waters of the wells become clean,
the waters of the sea become clean,
the standing waters become clean;
all the holy creatures,
the creatures of the good spirit,
become clean.

—ZEND-AVESTA

57

O God,
who divides the day from the night,
separate our deeds from the darkness of sin,
and let us continually live in your light,
reflecting in all that we do
your eternal beauty.

—LEONINE SACRAMENTARY

58

*I reverently speak in the presence
of the Great Parent God:
I pray that this day, the whole day,
as a child of God,
I may not be taken hold of by my own desire,
but show forth the divine glory
by living a life of creativeness,
which shows forth the true individual.*

—SHINTO PRAYER

59

Grant us, O Lord,
to pass this day in gladness and in peace,
without stumbling and without stain;
that, reaching the eventide victorious
over all temptation,
we may praise thee, the eternal God,
who art blessed, and dost govern all things,
world without end.

—MOZARABIC LITURGY

60

Father we thank Thee for the night,
And for the pleasant morning light;
For rest and food and loving care,
All that makes the day so fair.
Help us to do the things we should,
To be to others kind and good,
In all we do, in work or play,
To grow more loving every day.

—A CHILD'S MORNING PRAYER BY
  ABBIE C. MORROW

61

A certain day became a presence to me;
there it was, confronting me—
a sky, air, light: a being.
And before it started to descend
from the height of noon,
it leaned over and struck my shoulder
as if with the flat of a sword,
granting me honor and a task.
The day's blow rang out, metallic—
or it was I, a bell awakened,
and what I heard was my whole self
saying and singing what I knew:
I can.

—DENISE LEVERTOV

62

Earth our mother, breathe forth life
all night sleeping
now awaking
in the east
now see the dawn
Earth our mother, breathe and waken
leaves are stirring
all things moving
new day coming
life renewing
Eagle soaring, see the morning
see the new mysterious morning
something marvelous and sacred
though it happens every day
Dawn the child of God and Darkness

—PAWNEE PRAYER

63

Waking up this morning, I smile,
Twenty-four brand-new hours are before me.
I vow to live fully in each moment
and to look at all beings with eyes of
*   compassion.*

—THICH NHAT HANH

64

I arise today
Through the strength of heaven,
Light of sun,
Radiance of moon,
Splendor of fire,
Speed of lightning,
Swiftness of wind,
Depth of sea,
Stability of earth,
Firmness of rock.

—St. Patrick

65

I accept this new day as your gift,
and I enter it now with eagerness;
I open my senses to perceive you;
I lend my energies to things of goodness
    and joy.

—RITA SNOWDEN

66

O God, we pray this day:
for all who have a song they cannot sing,
for all who have a burden they cannot bear,
for all who live in chains they cannot break,
for all who wander homeless and cannot return,
for those who are sick and for those who tend
*   them,*
for those who wait for loved ones and wait
*   in vain,*
for those who live in hunger
and for those who will not share their bread,
for those who are misunderstood,
and for those who misunderstand,
for those who are captives
and for those who are captors,
for those whose words of love

are locked within their hearts
and for those who yearn to hear those words.
Have mercy upon these, O God.
Have mercy on us all.

—ANN WEEMS

Service

67

God, my friend,
is it possible to serve others
and not serve you?
I must remember that when
I look into the eyes of another,
I'm looking at you.
And when I help others,
I help myself,
and I help you.

—BRIAN WRIGHT

68

Dear God,
we shall have this day only once;
before it is gone,
help us to do all the good we can,
so that today is not a wasted day.

—STEPHEN GRELLET

69

*May my mouth praise
the love of God this morning.
O God, may I do your will this day.
May my ears hear the words of God
and obey them.
O God, may I do your will this day.
May my feet follow the footsteps of God
     this day.
O God, may I do your will this day.*

—JAPANESE PRAYER

70

I rise and pledge myself to God
to do no deed at all of dark.
This day shall be his sacrifice
and I, unmoved, my passion's Lord.
I blush to be so old and foul
and yet to stand before his table.
You know what I would do, O God;
O then, to do it make me able.

—GREGORY OF NAZIANZUS

71

Good morning, my friend God.
I give you the voyage of this day,
that to be, which is already yours,
adding to it my rejoicing,
a shout of praise. Amen. Amen.
You are the wind: fill up my sails.
You are the water: run fast beneath my keel.
And I will sing in the wind
and dance over the water,
God, my friend, oh God, my friend.
You are the light: enfold me.
You are the darkness: embrace me.
You are pain: hollow me.
You are love: overflow me.
The storms of change are you,
and the peace of tranquil waters.

You are all these things, Friend God,
and I thank you. Amen. Amen.
May I journey without fear
through all your seasons.
In emptiness let me find fullness.
In imprisonment let me find freedom.
Render me passive in your will
and I shall be most active,
moving with you in everything,
seeing you in everything,
knowing you in everything.
Amen. Amen.

—JOY COWLEY

72

My God, you are always close to me.
In obedience to you,
I must now apply myself to outward things.
Yet, as I do so,
I pray that you will give me
the grace of your presence.
And to this end I ask that you assist my work,
receive its fruits as an offering to you,
and all the while direct all my affections
*   to you.*

—BROTHER LAWRENCE

73

Oh, let me hear
Thy loving kindness in the morning,
for in Thee is my trust.
Teach me to do the thing that pleaseth Thee,
for Thou art my God.
Let Thy loving spirit lead me forth
into the land of righteousness.

—Bishop Lancelot Andrewes

74

Oh Lord, my God,
what is thy will for me today?
What task hast thou for me?
What opportunity hast thou placed in
     my way?
Open mine eyes that I may discover thy will!
Save me from wasting the new day!
May I turn it into eternal profit.

—JOHN H. JOWETT

75

At dawn and the opening of lotus buds,
my soul flower softly unfolds
to receive Thy light.
Each petal is bathed in rays of bliss.
The early breezes waft the perfume
of Thy presence.
Bless me, that with the spreading aurora
I spread to all men Thy message of love.
With the awakening day may I awaken
countless souls with my own
and bring them to Thee.

—Paramahansa Yogananda

76

The day returns and brings us
the petty round of irritating concerns
*   and duties.*
Help us to play the leader,
help us to perform them with laughter and
*   kind faces.*
Let cheerfulness abound with industry.
Give us to go blithely on our business all
*   this day,*
bring us to our resting beds
weary and content and undishonored,
and grant us in the end the gift of sleep.

—ROBERT LOUIS STEVENSON

77

Grant unto me, O Lord, that with peace
   of mind
I may face all that this new day is to bring.
Grant unto me to dedicate myself completely
to Thy Holy Will.
For every Hour of this day,
instruct and support me in all things.
Whatsoever tidings I may receive during
   the day,
do Thou teach me to accept tranquility,
in the firm conviction that all eventualities
   fulfill
Thy Holy Will.
Govern Thou my thoughts and feelings
in all I do and say.

When things unforeseen occur, let me
    not forget
that all cometh down from Thee.
Teach me to behave sincerely and rationally
toward every member of my family,
that I may bring confusion and sorrow
    to none.
Bestow upon me, my Lord,
strength to endure the fatigue of the day,
and to bear my part in all its passing events.
Guide Thou my will and teach me to pray,
to believe, to hope, to suffer, to forgive,
and to love.

—EASTERN ORTHODOX MEDITATION

78

Rule over me this day, O God,
leading me on the path of righteousness.
Put your Word in my mind
and your Truth in my heart,
that this day I neither think nor feel anything
except what is good and honest.
Protect me from all lies and falsehood,
helping me to discern deception wherever I
*   meet it.*
Let my eyes always look straight ahead
on the road you wish me to tread,
that I might not be tempted by any
*   distraction.*
And make my eyes pure,
that no false desires may be awakened within me.

—JAKOB BOEHME

Vision

79

God, my friend,
thoughts and pictures
fly through my mind unchecked.
Help me to focus
and hold my attention
on only those thoughts
which are useful
to both of us.

—BRIAN WRIGHT

80

Morning glory—
whose face
is without fault?

—LUCIEN STRYK

81

Let me not wander in vain.
Let me not labour in vain.
Let me not mingle with the prejudiced.
Let me not leave the company of the virtuous.
Let me not fly into anger.
Let me not stray off the path of goodness.
Let me not seek for this day or for the morrow.
Give me such a wealth, O Almighty!

—Pattinatar

82

Dear God,
Help me to take the common things of life
And make them beautiful.
Help me to do this today.
Let me not wait until tomorrow,
Or next week, or next summer for my joy;
Help me to find it today in the common task,
In accustomed places,
With the comrades of my home or workplace.

—RALPH SPAULDING CUSHMAN

83

Awake, O man, now is the break of day.
Thy life is running out like water from
*   thy palm.*
The bell ringeth out each hour;
the day that hath passed will not return.
The sun and moon warm thee;
thy life is drawing every day nearer to its end.
Know God within thyself.
Utter God's name alone,
and see Him in deep meditation.

— DADU

84

Brother,
the day hath broken,
Awake,
Remember thy God.

—SAHAJRAM

85

I am God's creature and my fellow is
*   God's creature.*
My work is in the town and his work is
in the country.
I rise early for my work and he rises early
for his work.
Just as he does not presume to do my work,
so I do not presume to do his work.
Will you say, I do much and he does little?
One may do much or one may do little;
it is all one,
provided he directs his heart to heaven.

— BERAKOTH

86

Grant that,
this day and every day,
we may keep our shock of wonder
at each new beauty that comes upon us
as we walk down the paths of life:
and that we may say in our hearts,
when horror and ugliness intervene,
Thy will be done.

—ANONYMOUS

87

We live in a world so strange,
That to live is only to dream.
He who lives, dreams his life
Until he wakes.
This much experience has taught me.

—PEDRO CALDERON DE LA BARCA

88

O God,
who brought me from the rest of last night
unto the joyous light of this day,
Be Thou bringing me from the new light of
*   this day*
Unto the guiding light of eternity.
Oh! from the new light of this day
unto the guiding light of eternity.

—GAELIC PRAYER

89

Bless to me, O God,
My soul and my body;
Bless to me, O God,
My belief and my condition;
Bless to me, O God,
My heart and my speech,
And bless to me, O God,
The handling of my hand;
Strength and busyness of morning,
Habit and temper of modesty,
Force and wisdom of thought,
And your own path, O God of virtues,
Till I go to sleep this night.

—TRADITIONAL CELTIC PRAYER

90

In the beginning was God,
Today is God,
Tomorrow will be God.
Who can make an image of God?
He has no body.
He is the word which comes out of your
  mouth.
That word! It is no more,
It is past, and still it lives!
So is God.

—AFRICAN PYGMY PRAYER

91

Cold, slow, silent, but returning,
after so many hours.
The sight of something outside me,
the day is breaking.
May salt, this one day, be sharp
upon my tongue;
May I sleep, this one night,
without waking.

—RANDALL JARRELL

92

Where the sun rises,
The Holy Young Man
The great plumed arrow
Has swallowed
And withdrawn it.
The sun
Is satisfied.

—AMERICAN INDIAN "SONG OF THE
    RISING SUN DANCE"

93

Wake!
For the sun who scatter'd into flight
The stars before him from the Field of Night,
Drives Night along with them from Heaven
and strikes the Sultan's Turret
with a Shaft of Light.

—FROM *THE RUBAIYAT OF OMAR KHAYYAM*

94

O friend,
awake, and sleep no more!
The night is over and gone,
would you lose your day also?

—KABIR

95

The Lord is my pace-setter, I shall not rush;
he makes me stop and rest for quiet intervals,
he provides me with images of stillness
which restore my serenity.
He leads me in the way of efficiency,
through calmness of mind;
and his guidance is peace.
Even though I have a great many things
to accomplish each day,
I will not fret, for his presence is here.
His timelessness, his all-importance
will keep me in balance.

He prepares refreshment and renewal
in the midst of activity,
by anointing my mind
with his oils of tranquility;
my cup of joyous energy overflows.
Surely harmony and effectiveness
shall be the fruits of my hours,
and I shall walk in the pace of my Lord,
and dwell in his house forever.

—"PSALM 23 FOR BUSY PEOPLE"
    BY TOKI MIYASHINA

96

Say to thyself, Marcus, at dawn:
today I shall run up against the busy-body,
the ungrateful, the overbearing, the deceitful,
the envious; the self-centered.
All this has fallen to their lot because
they are ignorant of good and evil.
But I, understanding the nature of the Good,
that it is fair, and of Evil, that it is ugly,
and the nature of the evil-doer himself,
that he is my kin—as sharing,
not indeed the same blood and seed,
but intelligence and a spark of the Divine—
can neither be damaged by any of them
(for no one can involve me in what is
    disgraceful)

nor can be angry with my kinsman
or estranged from him.
For we have been born for cooperation,
as have feet, hands, eyelids and the rows
of upper and lower teeth.
Therefore to thwart one another is unnatural;
and we do thwart one another
when we show resentment and dislike.

—MARCUS AURELIUS, ROMAN EMPEROR

97

The breezes at dawn have secrets to tell you.
Don't go back to sleep!
You must ask for what you really want!
Don't go back to sleep!
People are going back and forth
Across the doorsill where the two worlds
     touch;
The door is round and open.
Don't go back to sleep!

—RUMI

98

When a man has learnt
wisdom in the morning,
he may be content to die
in the evening before the sun sets.

—CONFUCIUS

99

Song of skylark—
night falls
from my face.

—LUCIEN STRYK

100

When at dawn, dale, hills, and bower
Shed the mist that on them lies,
And the chalice of the flower
Fills to charm our longing eyes;
When in ether clouds are carried
And with sunshine could contend,
When an east wind clouds has harried,
Give the sun pure thanks, admire
All his great and kindly powers:
Then with crimson flush he'll fire
Gold horizons as he lowers.

—GOETHE

101

Teach me thy love to know;
That this new light, which I now see,
May both the work and the workman show:
Then by a sunne-beam I will climb to thee.

—GEORGE HERBERT

102

O God,
who hast folded back the mantle of the night
to clothe us in the golden glory of the day,
chase from our hearts all gloomy thoughts,
and make us glad with the brightness of hope,
that we may effectively aspire to unwon
  virtues.

—AN ANCIENT COLLECTION, CA. 590 A.D.

Identifications

All of the entries in this book come from special people or cultures, yet my aim here is to provide notes of interest on historical, rather than contemporary, personalities and cultures. In some cases, such as with the entries from indigenous cultures, it proves very difficult to find adequate background information. The inclusion of entries in this section is therefore a product of historical records.

ENTRIES 3, 16, 44

The Tewa-Hopi are a tribe of the Pueblo Indians of the southwestern United States, specifically in Arizona and New Mexico.

ENTRY 6

The sutra is a short proverb or saying of Buddha (ca. 563–483 B.C.).There are many categories of sutras, one of which this entry is taken from.

ENTRY 11

The Armenian Church is easily one of the oldest branches of the Christian church, dating back to the work of the apostle St. Gregory the Illuminator, who is credited with converting King Tiridates III and several members of his court in A.D. 303.

ENTRY 12

This book of the Old Testament is sometimes called the Lamentations of Jeremiah, since he was widely held to be its author. It consists of five poems that were composed after the fall of Judah and the Babylonian destruction of the First Temple.

ENTRIES 13, 97

Jalal al-Din Muhammad Rumi (1207–73) was a Persian mystic and poet who followed the Islamic mystical movement called Sufism. Most of his copious writings were dedicated to his spiritual master, who disappeared without a trace in 1247. The Sufi sect called the Mevlevi, or whirling dervishes, is dedicated to the writings of Rumi and remains very active today, even in the West.

ENTRY 17

Tecumseh (1768–1813) was the leader of the Shawnee Indian tribe. Born in the area now known as Ohio, he fought against the white expansion into the Midwest and was killed in the battle of the Thames, near Thamesville, Ontario.

ENTRY 21

The Koran, or Qur'an, is the earliest known work in Arabic prose. There are many versions known but only one authorised version, which was first published around A.D. 650. The 114 chapters of the Koran contain the Islamic religious, social, civil, commercial, military, and legal codes.

ENTRY 22

Edward Estlin Cummings (1894–1962) is loved as one of the most inventive and experimental American writers of the twentieth century. One of the distinct features of his work is the lack of uppercase letters (he preferred e.e. cummings until the 1930s). Other characteristics include a jazz-like rhythm, distorted syntax, and odd punctuation. He wrote most often about the value of love.

ENTRY 26

The Rig-Veda is the first of the four Vedas, a series of ancient sacred Indian texts that were first written in Vedic, an early form of Sanskrit. It consists of over a thousand hymns composed in different poetic meters and separated into ten volumes. The Vedas are believed to have originated between 1300 and 1000 B.C. The vedas in their present form are believed to date from the third century B.C.

ENTRY 30

Rudolf Steiner (1861–1925) was an Austrian-born philosopher and scientist who founded the spiritual-scientific movement called anthro-posophy. A prolific lecturer and writer, his work is still being translated and edited today, and his many initiatives, such as the Waldorf schools and biodynamic agriculture, continue to grow in popularity.

ENTRY 31

John Henry Newman (1801–90) was an English clergyman and a leader of the Oxford movement. An outstanding essayist in his day, he wrote the hymn "Lead Kindly Light" while touring the Mediterranean.

ENTRY 33

Soren Kierkegaard (1813–55) was a Danish philosopher. His ideas focused around existentialism and the meaning of choices. His work profoundly influenced the theology of his day.

ENTRIES 34, 78

Jakob Boehme (1575–1624), a German shoemaker by trade, was a passionate Christian mystic who sought direct divine illuminations. His writings and lectures appealed to both the Evangelical Church and to scientists such as Hegel and Newton, making him a true pioneer in Western metaphysical thought.

ENTRY 36

The Druze are a Muslim sect based in the mountainous regions of Labanon and southern Syria. Originating around the eleventh century, their faith is an outgrowth of Islam, but with elements of Christianity and Judaism.

ENTRY 48

Dietrich Bonhoeffer (1906–45), was a German Lutheran theologian. This particular entry is his last recorded prayer. It was said just hours before he was hanged in a concentration camp by the Nazis for his opposition to the party and to anti-Semitism.

ENTRY 56

The Zend-Avesta is the prayer book of Zoroastrianism. Its present-day followers are known as Parsis and reside in Iran, India, and Pakistan.

ENTRY 57

The Leonine Sacramentary is traditionally credited in part to St. Gelasius, pope from 492 to 496. This compilation of letters is believed to have been published in the sixth century.

ENTRY 58

Shinto means "the way of the gods" in Japanese. The Shinto religion began around the sixth century A.D. However, it was quickly overshadowed by Buddhism and Confucianism and did not emerge again until the eighteenth century, when it was revived as the official national religion of Japan.

ENTRY 59

The Mozarabic liturgy was the official liturgy of the church of Spain from the sixth through the twelfth centuries and is now found only in the Spanish city of Toledo.

ENTRY 64

St. Patrick (389–461) is often called the Apostle of Ireland. It is said that the shamrock, the Irish national symbol, can be traced back to his use of it as an illustration of the trinity.

ENTRY 70

St. Gregory of Nazianzus (330–389) was one of the four Eastern Doctors of the Christian church and spent most of his life in the area now known as Turkey. Along with countless sermons and letters, he wrote many poems dealing with morality.

ENTRY 72

Brother Lawrence (1605–91), originally named Nicholas Herman, was born in France and spent his early years as a soldier of the Holy Roman Empire. In his later years, he joined a monastary and became a well-known Christian mystic and writer. His most important work was called *The Practice of the Presence of God.*

ENTRY 73

Bishop Lancelot Andrewes (1555–1626) was an English theologian who took a distinctively Anglican approach to his interpretations of the Bible. He was widely regarded as one of the most learned men in England during his later years.

ENTRY 75

Paramahansa Yogananda was an Indian Yogi who brought his teachings to the West in the 1920s and subsequently established a center in southern California called the Self-Realization Fellowship, which is still very active today. His book *Autobiography of a Yogi* is a perennial bestseller.

ENTRY 76

Robert Louis Stevenson (1850–94) was a Scottish novelist and poet who contributed much to the dreams and imaginations of children of all ages. Some of his most famous works are *Treasure Island*, *The Strange Case of Dr. Jekyll and Mr. Hyde*, and *Kidnapped*.

ENTRY 83

Dadu (1544–1603) was a Hindu religious reformer and poet.

ENTRY 87

Pedro Calderon de la Barca (1600–81) was a Spanish poet and dramatist and is considered one of the most prominent figures in Spain's literary golden age.

ENTRY 91

Randall Jarrell (1914–65) was an American poet and author of several children's books.

ENTRY 93

The *Rubaiyat* is a poem written by the Persian poet Omar Khayyam. It was translated into English by Edward Fitzgerald and published in the West in 1859.

ENTRY 94

Kabir (1440–1518), an Indian poet and mystic, formed the bhakti (passionate devotion) movement of Hinduism. He later found a strong connection to the Islamic mystical religion of Sufism, which drew much protest from the fundamentalists of both groups.

ENTRY 96

Marcus Aurelius (121–180) was the emperor of Rome from 161 to 180. He was also a philosopher of stoicism, which stresses moderation, morality, and justice.

ENTRY 98

Confucius (551–479) was a Chinese philosopher and easily the most consistently noteworthy figure in Chinese culture and history. His teachings, which were highly practical and ethical, made him a much-revered spiritual teacher, though he himself had little belief in a supernatural God.

ENTRY 100

Johann Wolfgang von Goethe (1749–1832) was a German poet, dramatist, novelist, and scientist. He was able to reflect his unique understanding of man's connection with nature through all of his disciplines and skills. His most famous work, *Faust*, is about a man who sells his soul to the devil in exchange for the power to cure his village of the plague.

ENTRY 101

George Herbert (1593–1633) was a Welsh poet and metaphysician. He later became a priest with the Church of England. His unique use of imagery and meter in his poetry was an influence on later poets, such as John Donne, of the metaphysical school.

Acknowledgments

Entries 4, 15, 37, and 90 from *An African Prayer Book* by Desmond Tutu. Copyright 1995 by Desmond Tutu. Used by permission of Doubleday, a division of Bantam Doubleday Dell Publishing Group, Inc.

Entry 20 from *American Indian Prayers and Poetry* by J. Ed Sharpe. Copyright 1985 by Cherokee Publications, Box 256, Cherokee, North Carolina 28719. Used by permission of the publisher.

Entry 61 from *Breathing the Water* by Denise Levertov. Copyright 1987 by Denise Levertov. Reprinted by permission of New Directions Publishing Corp.

Entry 53 from The Society for Promoting Christian Knowledge. Holy Trinity Church, Marylebone Road, London, England NW1 4DU. Used by permission.

Entries 3, 16, and 44 from *Songs of the Tewa* by Herbert J. Spinden, courtesy of Sunstone Press, Box 2321, Santa Fe, New Mexico 87504-2321.

Entries 80 and 99 from *And Still Birds Sing* by Lucien Stryk. Copyright 1998 by Swallow Press. Used by permission of the author.

Entries 30 and 50 from *Verses and Meditations* by Rudolf Steiner. Copyright 1979 by Rudolf Steiner Press, London, England. Reprinted by permission of the publisher.

Entry 75 from *Whispers from Eternity* by Paramahansa Yogananda. Copyright 1986 by Self-Realization Fellowship, Los Angeles, California.

Entry 10 from *You Must Be Joking, Lord* by Michael Hollings and Etta Gullick. Published by McCrimmon Publishing Co., Ltd. Reprinted by permission of the publisher.

About the Editor

BRIAN WRIGHT is a writer and media producer who has been interested in spiritual development and religious practices since childhood. He lives in Minneapolis. He is also the editor of *Meeting the Night: Bedtime Prayers and Meditations from Around the World*, published by Adams Media.